Petals

in the Sun...
Remembering You

Poetry That Honors Your Past, Comforts Your Present,
and Lights Your Way Toward Healing and Peace

by Darlene PR

34 Poems & Lined Journal

Petals in the Sun... Remembering You

Poetry That Honors Your Past, Comforts Your Present,
and Lights Your Way Toward Healing and Peace

Author/Publisher Contact:
Darlene PR, DK Pages
P.O. Box 630343
Lanai City, HI 96763

ISBN 979-8-9882236-4-1 (eBook)
ISBN 979-8-9882236-6-5 (Hardcover)
ISBN 979-8-9882236-5-8 (Paperback)

Library of Congress Control Number: 2025911708

Printed in the United States of America
First Edition: July 2025

Dedications

To all...
Find your quiet place, play soothing music,
this moment is for you. Journal pages in back.

To my late husband of years ago...
Remembering you.

Contents

Sunshine for You

At the end

of the night

and the dawn

of a new day,

the sun will

once again

shine your way.

Whispering Winds

Starlight in the evening sky
illuminates an angel by your side.
Night will be very long
calling for its wind-chime song.

As echoes blow
in whispering winds,
the cool air
will softly sing.

Heart of the sky
shield brother's light,
a guardian angel is by your side
through this very night.

*"Heaven,
there's an angel
by your side..."*

Heaven's Garden

In Heaven, there's a special place
where flowers grow
entwined with lace,
made for you with
loving grace
beyond
Heaven's gates.

Seeds I've planted
now in bloom
bear the fruits
of a radiant you.
Angels will
rejoice everywhere
as I lift and take you there.

In glory and in
peaceful rest,
cherished memories,
children blessed,
your garden awaits with
nurturing embrace
in Heaven's special place.

Cavandish Golf Course, Lāna'i

In the Clearing

At the edge of the path
before evening,
we pause by a rose in the clearing.
On the hill, he points as he takes a glance,
knowing I'd understand.

Taking in the beauty of
the golfer's hillside,
he looks toward the sky.
There stand the island pines
towering up high.

In the distance, a golfer plays
between the ironwoods and pines,
near the end of a golfer's day.
In awe at the views,
he sighs.

A final look
in these very surroundings,
his journey here is complete.
He is...
forever at peace.

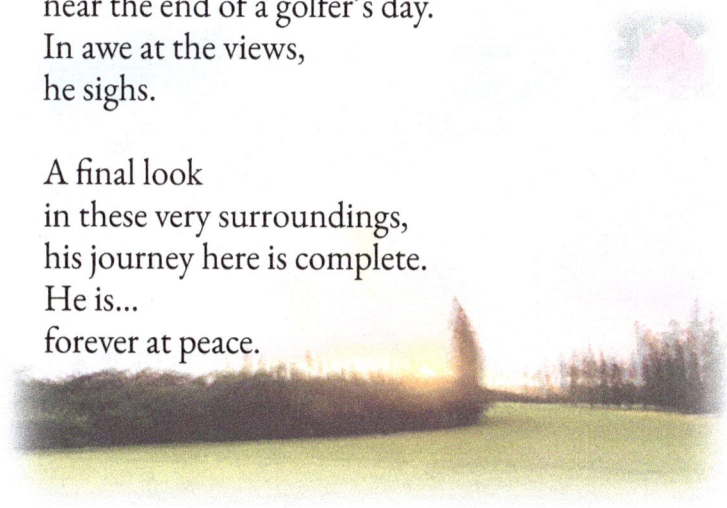

Butterfly of Mine

Searching everywhere,
in your mind, I'm there,
see me in your dreams
while sleeping.

Butterfly of mine,
fly with me through time
and soar among the clouds
while dreaming.

Rest your head in prayer,
know that I will be
purple hues in the light
of your dreams.

Butterfly of mine,
sleep peacefully tonight,
the breeze will guide your wings
till daylight.

Flying everywhere,
I'll be with you there,
endless is the bond
we'll forever share.

Butterfly of mine,
fly with me through time
and soar among
the heavens divine.

By My Side

By my side, you follow.
By my side, you lead.
By my side, the anchor is of you.

The rhythm of the islands' calling
fast upon the shores.
The ocean waves come rolling...
hear them calling out your name.

Your breath is in the winds and flying
high above the sea.
Your presence in the air, I feel—
the essence of you near.

The ocean full of life surrounds me,
stars in harmony.
Loved ones and ancestors are near,
I feel their spirits with you here.

By my side, you follow.
By my side, you lead.
By my side, the anchor is of you.

By my side, you follow.
By my side, you lead.
By my side, the anchor is of you.

Hahai ʻoe, ma koʻu ʻaoʻao.
Kaʻi ʻoe, ma koʻu ʻaoʻao.
ʻO ka heleuma ʻoe, ma koʻu ʻaoʻao.

Gem

In the early morning light,
feel the warmth of calm from night
with illuminating colors
in the twilight of your smile.

Gem of amethyst-colored wings,
the glow of you will always be
a light of love and faith
throughout eternity.

In my heart you're always there—
in my thoughts and everywhere.
I walk around and feel a part of you
among places we've been to.

Gem, I see, illuminating
in the light past dawn,
you'll forever be
a precious gem.

Your Smile

My dearest friend,
as I held your hand,
with your last breath, you smiled.

You were comforted
as you closed your eyes
and let go of this time.

Your soul now rests
in a peaceful place
where we will meet again one day.

I love you, and I believe
we will always have each other
in the memories we keep.

I smile because you smiled
and are now smiling
down from Heaven.

Forever Young

I am blessed
to have had you in my life.
I looked up to you while growing up.

You have made my life
impressionable,
in ways that only you could.

Young, you were
when you passed away so suddenly.
You were so dear to me.

But unexpected circumstances of
an accident, an illness, an enduring pain,
happened to take the lead.

Wherever I go,
whatever I do,
my champion will always be you.

Fond memories,
I hold on to,
forever with me... forever you.

Storybook Dreams

I never got to hold you.
I never got to sing you a lullaby.
You never had a name.

Years later, I wrote a story
and turned to my book.
I then realized,
I then understood.

I finally got to hold you in the pages.
I finally got to sing you a fairy-tale song.
You finally had a name.

Truly, the most adorable little child
who laughs and plays
and dances and sings
in the world of storybook dreams.

Always Within

As long as I am breathing
and my heart goes on beating,
you will always live within.

Love in My Pockets

My love for you has never died.
It simply melded into existence,
tucked away
in the pockets of my mind.

Your love for me has never died.
You loved me unconditionally,
again and again, one by one,
till it filled the pockets of my mind.

Our love has never died.
I broke the rules and said goodbye
to my life, to follow you
through life.

Lost love has never died.
Although you have departed,
images of you play on and on
in the pockets of my mind.

A love that never dies
is, I believe,
the greatest love of all,
now kept in the pockets of my mind.

And We Danced

A slow song played,
you came my way,
we danced in synchronous
rhythm and sway.
A magical dream of holding you
in perfect alignment... we two.

Then came uneasiness
and unrest.
I opened my eyes and cried.
Taken aback, I realized
the dream had spoken...
your dance was goodbye.

Awakened in sadness and solitude,
I held myself, dancing alone.
In the darkness of the night
and the stillness of the cold,
sorrow struck my world...
the story became silent and left untold.

You were not here.
You never came back.
You were nowhere around.
You were gone.
Minutes seemed like hours,
counted one by one.

But then, I collapsed
into a dream—
spiraling in a magical trance.
Upon Heaven's carousel,
I found you...
and we danced.

Yesterday's Sorrow

Yesterday's sorrow
trickles within.
It leaks through the seams,
overflows in the air,
drips over everything.

A cold front is coming
below the skies of blue.
The clouds are ever-changing,
they keep on shifting,
they keep moving on.

If not today,
then tomorrow,
will loneliness shift,
will sadness move on
like the clouds do every day?

Time will make it easier,
believe in faith and prayer.
Your heart will fill
with laughter
once again.

If not today,
then tomorrow,
say bye to yesterday's sorrow...
you will,
and so will I.

Paw Prints

When I first saw you, I picked you up
and gave you a great big hug.
I knew you'd be mine forever,
then came paw prints on the door.

Every day, you'd wait for me.
Every day, you'd follow me.
Every day, you'd sit by me.
Paw prints here and there, I'd see.

Every day was jump and play.
For treats, you'd eagerly run my way!
Sometimes you'd give paw shakes and stay.
Sometimes you'd sneak and run away!

The years with you went by quickly.
As time went on, you'd move slowly.
Most days you'd rest under a shady tree
and wag your tail longingly.

I noticed, more than ever, that you needed me.
When you'd put your head on my lap gently,
I'd hug and soothe you lovingly.
Paw prints everywhere, I'd see.

Always there, my faithful friend,
always there till the very end.
No waiting and following me anymore.
Paw prints now on Heaven's door.

Forever kept in memory...
Paw prints left by you, I'd see.

Colors in Flight

Colors of you
seen in colors of me.
Wings in the moonlight
of colors in flight.

Colors of me
seen in colors of you,
golden red and blue
in purple's bright hues.

Colors flowing through,
as vibrant as the stars at night,
in colors of you
and colors of me in flight.

Dear Sister

I remember us.
I thought it would always be us,
but the years went by fast...
we grew up.

I didn't feel the impact
until years later,
after we went our own ways
and lived separate lives.

We will never cross this path again
in this lifetime,
as we did while growing up.
I will always treasure those times.

When I reflect on our childhood years,
I wouldn't have wanted it any other way.
I love you, dear sister...
and sisters x two.

His Silence

On the road, he walked.
The town he grew up in
burned to ashes all around.
What he saw was so heartbreaking.
He kept silent, but his eyes showed grief.
Sorrow laid heavily on his mind,
his pain was so great.
Words remained on his tongue for a while,
nothing was spoken at all,
as the scenes of the fire played on and on.

But his quietness spoke loudly
in shouts of sadness and despair.
Across the ocean, I felt his pain.
He silently called their names and prayed,
to help bring them home,
and help them find their way
to rest in peace
in a serene and heavenly place.

"His silence," dear brother... was you.
I heard you across the ocean tides that swirled,
crying out your name...
and the world grieved with all of you.

Lahaina, Maui – harbor area years before.

Rest in Beautiful Calm

Give me a story, o Moloka'i... tell me a story of old.
Share your history where we connect
to our ancestors of long ago,
in a little place hidden from the world.

You embraced a life so confined, yet in some way,
hopefully free, I would want to believe.
In my writing, I want to share
a piece of my heart with you.

Because of you, we are here in this life.
Because of you, we live.
Our lives would've never been,
if it weren't for you.

You sacrificed for us
when you were taken to Kalaupapa,
where you remained
for the rest of your years.

Your Hawaiian homelands, your past,
and those you knew became frozen in time.
No longer to live with your ohana (–family),
your memories dissipated like mist after dawn.

It changed your lives and, in turn,
it changed our lives too.
But know that a part of you
will always be in our hearts.

Oh, come, our Hawaiian ancestors.
Rest in peace in the history of you
and those who were brought
there long ago.

May we take comfort in knowing
that you are in a place
surrounded by beautiful calm—
part of an ancestor's home.

Rest in peace, our ancestors...
                rest in beautiful calm.

Give me a story, o Molokaʻi...
                tell me a story of old.

Kalaupapa, Moloka'i

Lānaʻi, Hawaiʻi

Island Home

Pine trees rustle
in a hush of humming calls.
Branches bend
towards a gracious fall,
as if ancestors are reaching down,
embracing us all.

Of old ones before us...
they lived the stories,
then Heaven called.
Of young ones now...
we weave new stories
as we carry on.

A trace of you, a trace of me on
dirt roads, on sand,
on paths of steppingstones—we
become part of history
on the island
we call home.

Island of Lāna'i, Hawai'i

Leaf

A leaf has fallen
 to the ground,
  withered and
   weathered
    to dirt and dust,
     giving all that was.

Like a leaf that
 fed the ground,
  seeds of earth,
   a new plant formed.
    From you,
     a new life born.

Kekulamamo
Golden mamo birds of past
Yellow feathers cloaked.

Haiku

Night Sky's Calling

The daylight is ending,
the evening is setting
upon you.

The winds are shifting,
the breeze is stirring
around you.

See the sun going down,
its warmth will see
you through.

See the ocean far beyond,
it's sending
blessings too,
in everlasting breaths
for you.

The night sky is calling,
the night stars are falling
upon you.

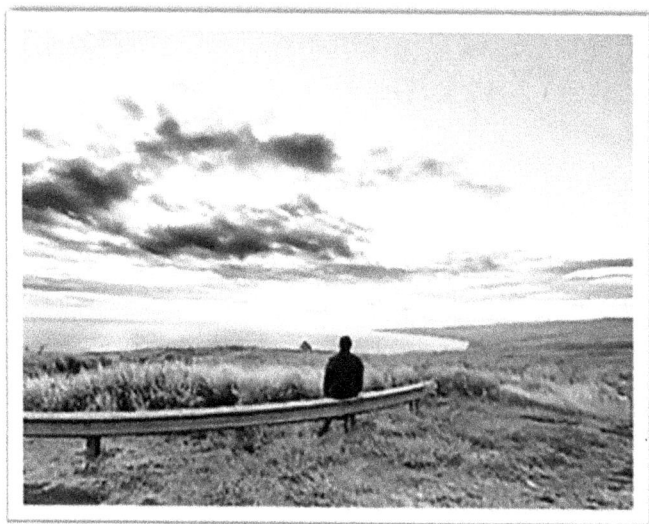

The night sky is aligning
with the night stars forming
around you.

See the light in the dark,
it's shining just
for you.

See the tears fall from the clouds,
they're smiling rain
on you...
in everlasting breaths
for you.

One Day, One July

The heavens are shining
with the beautiful presence of you.
The skies are radiating with the
warmth of your laughter and smile.

In moments of sadness, I sometimes
ask myself why and what if.
A teardrop falls.
I quietly grieve.

Then I imagine you in a
veil that brings your spirit through.
Will you remember me?
Will you remember my name?

I'd open up the heavens to see you again.
If I could, I would.
If not close by, then from a distance,
I would watch as you walk by.

Maybe one day. Maybe one July...

Bittersweet Laced in Teal

It must have been in my dreams,
in my view, surreal,
the feeling of you near,
bittersweet nights in teal.

It must have been in my view,
so near, so true,
the presence of you here,
bittersweetness in tears.

It must have been what I've seen,
with you here, so real,
the vision is so clear,
bittersweet laced in teal.

If Forever

If forever is eternity,
let the stars show me a sign.
Let the night sky fall upon my hands
and guide me through this time.

Little One

One night, my little one, then three, waved
into the air
and smiled so happily.
I asked, "Son, what do you see?"
He replied, "It's daddy!
He's waving to me."

I looked around, then asked, "Where is he?"
My little son pointed towards the door.
"Look, he's right there, mommy.
Daddy's happy to see me."
I tried hard to see
what only he could see.

After a moment, he said,
"Daddy's leaving now."
I watched my little one
wave into the air and smile so happily.
I held back my tears, hoping to see
what only he could see.

That night, his daddy came by
before the long goodbye.
Soon after, his little son fell asleep peacefully.
His daddy came to see
his little one, then three,
little Anthony.

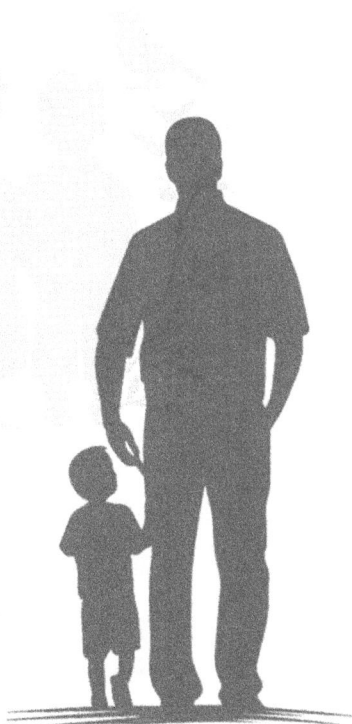

Fly Beyond

Far beyond,
visions soar.

Listen to voices
calling your name.

Take flight like a phoenix—
your dream begins...

Feel it in your wings
and fly!

Heaven

Heaven, there's an

    angel by your side.

        Kindly give her

            all my love.

Heaven, there's a

    gentle soul with you.

        Please send him

            all my love.

Heaven, shelter them

with open arms.

Heaven, shelter them

with all your love.

Rhythm of a Heartbeat

Listen to your heartbeat,
it's playing a song.

It beats for you in rhythm,
all day and all night long.
Although it remains hidden,
it strums for you in song.

Like a melody that never ends,
wherever you go, it will be—
playing rhythms in harmony,
playing rhythms in beats.

Intertwined with another soul,
your heartbeats blend.
You beat to the same drummer,
you beat to the same sounds.

When one is gone,
the heart of the other lives on
and beats to the rhythm
of two souls.

Listen to your heartbeat,
it's playing your song.

Feathers from Heaven

The sun sets
in the west,
tracing the contours
of their feathers
to the tips of their wings.

The sun sets
beyond the water's edge,
radiating toward the heavens.
Stunning colors
of angel birds in flight.

I Miss You

The fire burns deeply.
The cold wind is at peace.
The embers spark memories of you.

I miss you.

You Will Remember

A time will come one day
when you will remember
the features of a face,
the essence of a smile.

You will wake from a dream,
feel the sun break its peace,
hear a voice in the breeze,
see a smile in the trees.

This feeling will not hide
the aura by your side.
Breathe, just breathe for a time...
reminisce for a while.

By the Way

By

The

Way...

Looking out

The window,

I found

    Sunshine,

        And I'm

            Sending it

                Your way.

Poem Information

Pages 65-70

About Several Poems

Whispering Winds, p. 9
Starlight... my youngest—a bright light in life. Heart of the sky...
my firstborn—the heart of the family. This poem reflects mourning
a recent loss.

Heaven's Garden, p. 11
I wrote this after my mom, Margaret Pagay Vea, passed away. She
lived a full, happy life. This poem is also tied to departed uncles,
aunts, parents, and grandparents. For anyone needing comfort and
reassurance, this poem is for you.

In the Clearing, p. 13
One afternoon, I rode around the Cavendish golf course with my
dad, Deason Dodge Baybayan, a few months before Heaven called.
Dolly's rose was growing by the clearing.

Butterfly of Mine, p. 14
Lyrics of a song I wrote for my daughter-in-law, Michelle Fujie-
Kaauamo, and her family, after her loving mom departed. Sharing
the poem version.

By My Side, p. 16
I wrote this song after a cousin, Chad Kalepa Baybayan, passed
away unexpectedly. He was a Pwo master navigator of the Hawaiian
voyage canoe, *Hōkūle'a*. Written with two beautiful ladies in
mind—his wife, Audrey Kaide Baybayan, and his mom,

Lillian Kalepa Suter. This poem extends to everyone who loves the ocean and canoeing. Hawaiian translation of song chorus, p. 17

Gem, p. 18
Gem came to me in melody as I thought about a cousin, Charlene Pidot-Buchner, who passed away from an illness. Written in poetry setting for all to embrace.

Your Smile, p. 20
A poem for those who have experienced loss of a friend or loved one from cancer, disease, illness, or related. You will meet again someday. Blessings to you.

Forever Young, p. 21
Written about those who have passed away as young adults. Dying young, they never got to experience their lives fully. Love to all.

Storybook Dreams, p. 22
Written about those who were never born. For the parents and families who have experienced such great loss, the "storybook" is your story, your song, and your dream in the way you believe it to be.

And We Danced, p. 26
A life taken. He came by, and we danced that night. I found out the day after, that my husband passed away hours before he appeared to me. In spirit, he gave me the dance we always talked about. The dance calmed my soul.

Paw Prints, p. 30

For the love of pets and animals... blessings to all of you. Your pets and animals have touched your lives in so many ways. The memories you keep of your loving friends remain with you forever. Paws or no paws, my heart goes out to you.

Dear Sister, p. 33

My sister I grew up with, Viola Baybayan-Fabrao. Love Tita, Gina.

His Silence, p. 34

Prayers and comfort to all of the Lahaina people, relatives, friends, and those who experienced great loss from the fire. Written with my brothers in mind: Dodgie, Kawai, Kaleo, and Keith.

Rest in Beautiful Calm, p. 36

Kalaupapa is a peninsula on the north side of Moloka'i, where a colony was established in 1866 for people who were sent there after being diagnosed with Hansen's Disease—leprosy. Love to you all.

Island Home, p. 41

Island of Lāna'i—home. For the love of the people, for the love of the island, this one's for you and me.

Haiku Poem - no title, p. 43

Kekulamamo means Golden Mamo Bird—a name given to me by my Hawaiian grandmother, Ellen Kaauamo Baybayan. The mamo birds' feathers were black with some yellow and white. The gold 'ahu'ula (feather cloak) of King Kamehameha I, was made entirely from the yellow feathers of the mamo birds.

One Day, One July, p. 46
A piece of writing to my late husband.

Bittersweet Laced in Teal, p. 48
Originally written as a song about my youngest son, Sheldon, who was far away when he endured medical complications and was hospitalized with Covid. The sweetness of his inner being and the bitterness of pain—bittersweet. Love to you, son. This extends to all survivors of Covid and other serious illnesses.

Little One, p. 50
This happened to my firstborn, Anthony, at age three. For the love of a son and his father, the bond will always be. Love you, son.

Feathers from Heaven, p. 59
All birds and animals are special. When Heaven calls, angels guide them on their way back home. Images of feathers in the evening's sky resemble feathers from Heaven.

I Miss You, p. 60
I miss you.

Pictures by Darlene

p. 11 and Book Cover: Garden sunflowers.

pp. 12-13: Section of the golf course from top of hill.

p. 35: A section of Lahaina Harbor years ago.

p. 39: Kalaupapa, Moloka'i, from a lookout above.

pp. 40-41: Pictures of Lāna'i from Moloka'i, by Valerie Nanod Gonzalez. Pine tree photo by Darlene.

p. 45: Anthony watching the Lāna'i sunset, ocean in the distance.

p. 55: Michelle and Anthony looking toward the heavens.

p. 60: Sitting by a fire on a winter's night, picture taken by A.K.

Other: Watercolor prints, owned; outlays, purchased.

Songs in Poetry Form
by Darlene

Bittersweet Laced in Teal

Butterfly of Mine

By My Side

Colors in Flight

Gem

Heaven

Night Sky's Calling

About The Author

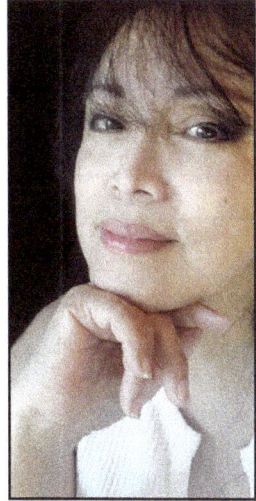

Darlene is a poet, author, and artist from the island of Lānaʻi, Hawaiʻi. She is expanding her repertoire from children's books to poetry for an adult audience.

Darlene's poetry book *Petals in the Sun... Remembering You* is written in a simple, traditional, and free-verse style. She touches on themes of love, loss, grief, and faith, in hopes that her words will help others feel understood and less alone in their own journeys.

Her poems are meant to bring comfort to anyone who has lost or said goodbye to someone they love and is searching for light during a difficult time. In poetry form, Darlene opens a window into some of her experiences.

Prior to her recent creative endeavors, some of her work included education, luxury resorts, and retail management. Although her professional journey has been diverse, poetry has always been at the center of her heart.

In her free time, Darlene takes pleasure in birdwatching while enjoying music and taking in the sounds of nature. She finds peace in the simple, melodic moments of life.

JOURNAL

Lined pages to write thoughts, poems, songs,
draw, add pictures, and more.

_____

_____

_____

_____

_____

_____

_____

_____

_____

_____

_____

_____

_____

_____

_____

_____

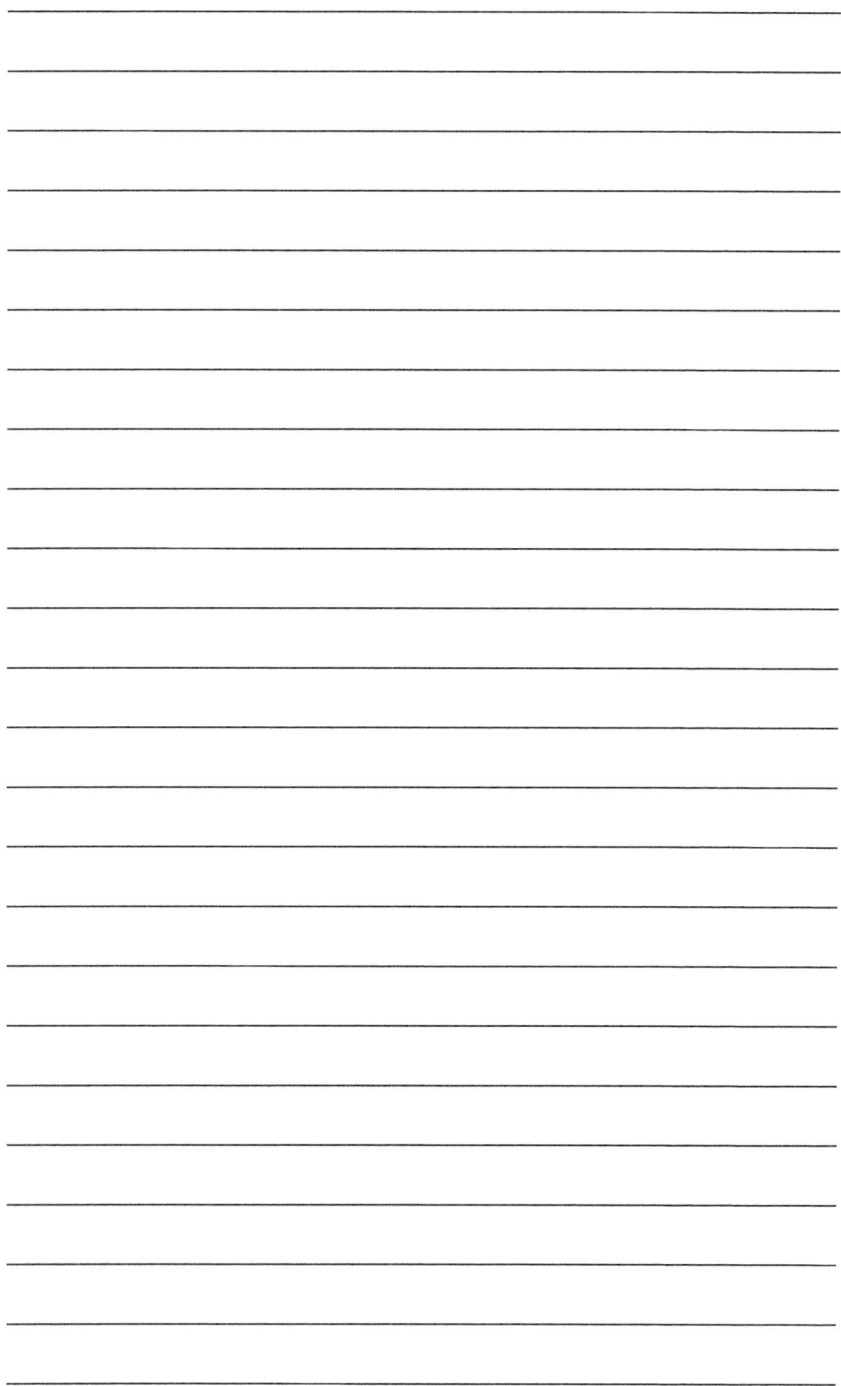

www.ingramcontent.com/pod-product-compliance
Lightning Source LLC
Chambersburg PA
CBHW062025040426
42447CB00010B/2139